WHISPERS OF BROKEN

TRUST

WHISPERS OF BROKEN
TRUST
The Painful Truth of Child Abuse

Suffering motivates us to change our behavior whenever possible, to enhance our chances of survival.

"You broke my heart, my body, and my pride; you left behind scars that lasted a lifetime, but you could never break my spirit and enduring will to survive.

A Book by

Tamara Rivera

Printed in the United States of America

ISBN 979-8-89114-131-5 (hc)
ISBN 979-8-89114-130-8 (sc)
ISBN 979-8-89114-132-2 (e)

Library of Congress Control Number: 2024921838

2025.02.17

MainSpring Books
5901 W. Century Blvd
Suite 750
Los Angeles, CA, US, 90045

www.mainspringbooks.com

INTRODUCTION

Dear reader, dive into a reality that so many of us know but rarely speak aloud—the lingering impact of broken promises and shattered faith. This book uncovers the often-hidden world of trust betrayed and the quiet strength required to rebuild our inner worlds after facing such circumstances.

Through these pages, I share my own story of navigating betrayal, isolation, and self-discovery, not just as a transgender woman but as a human being learning to trust again after enduring such hardships. This journey has been one of piecing together my identity and reclaiming my power despite the scars of the past.

My hope is that *Whispers of Broken Trust* speak to anyone who has felt abandoned, deceived, or forgotten. It is a testament to the resilience we carry within us, even when life feels like it's crumbling. May these words inspire you to believe in yourself once more, to find strength in vulnerability, and to rediscover trust where it feels lost.

Welcome to a journey of healing—welcome to *Whispers of Broken Trust*.

CONTENTS

DEDICATION

I endured a lifetime of pain and suffering on my journey. For 59 years, I had a dream, and I never gave up. Regrettably, this was not a viable alternative. I had my hopes and dreams shattered, but I never considered that becoming a woman was a lost dream; I held on and accomplished my dream and lived to share it with you.

The dedication of this book goes to the amazing people who supported me on my journey. One day, while talking to my friend Nannette on Facebook, I shared parts of my story. She encouraged me to write a book.

I survived the horrible truth of child abuse, and this is my story. I hope it touches your heart and inspires you.

With sincere love,

Tamara Rivera

PREFACE

Parents often believe they have complete authority over their children and see themselves as being above the law. Why is this? Parents who feel threatened by losing control may become furious with their children, behaving like angry bulls. Certain parents take a dictatorial approach, using any means necessary to maintain control over their children.

In the early days of my childhood in Puerto Rico, child abuse prevailed with alarming frequency. Whether at home, school, or even in public settings, children endured abuse, and this dark reality remained largely unreported.

The distressing aspect was the reluctance of anyone to intervene or stop the abuse. Children were at the mercy of parents, educators, and other authority figures who harshly punish them with no way to defend themselves. People didn't believe them and thought they were imagining things or didn't understand.

I don't have statistics, but my personal experience as a child with an abusive father and teachers who faced no consequences illustrates this concerning issue.

I aspire to be straightforward without sugar-coating. I researched the characteristics of an abusive parent. Here are unmistakable signs of child abuse in a child's home.

Act now to prevent childhood and teenage hardships. Painful memories are difficult to forget. Just like formatting a hard drive, trying to forget doesn't erase the pain completely.

CHAPTER ONE
DID I DESERVE THIS?

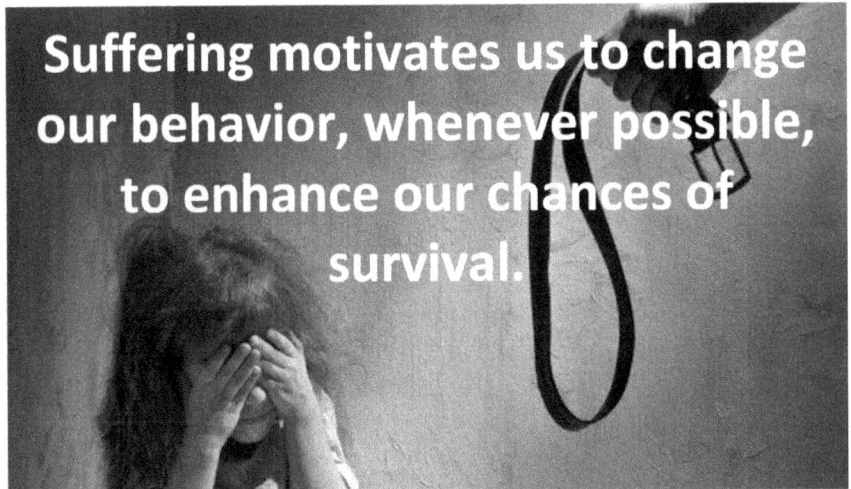

Suffering motivates us to change our behavior, whenever possible, to enhance our chances of survival.

"Child abuse is an horrific experience with potentially lasting effects. Unfortunately, It's also a common occurrence around the world".

My father was a beast disguised as a human who sought every opportunity to inflict pain and suffering and casually carried on a conversation with his friends like it had never happened.

As I sat in a corner away from his view, I thought, how can you abuse a child and then laugh it off as if nothing happened? It was only an excuse for his behavior; He would justify his behavior by saying that it's what a father must do to keep it all under control and have some respect from his children. I can't believe that was his frame of thought, that it's what he must do to instill respect in his children.

My oldest sister was born in New York in March 1961, and I was born in 1962, in Rio Piedras, Puerto Rico; I'm the second child of six. I lived my first year in Puerto Rico with my Aunt Lidia while my parents settled in Chicago, Illinois. My aunt took me to my parents in Chicago, where we lived until I was ten. My father was employed at Kellogg's in 1963.

Growing up in Chicago, I remember the old house we lived in, an avocado green two-story home with a basement, a separate garage on the back of the house on to the left side, and a long gravel driveway leading to the barn-style garage; I remember an old 1930s rusted Ford that I wondered why it was there but never asked. There were old rusted garden tools and a tractor plow and behind the garage there were a few cotton plants and other items I never knew what they were.

The house seemed big from my point of view. I don't remember how many rooms it had, but I remember that as you walked into the front of the house, there was a long sidewalk leading to the steps up to the full-length front porch. As you walked up to the house, to the right there was an apple tree. The front yard was significant; the front door had the bottom half in wood and the top half in glass squares, and once you walked inside, the steps to the upper level faced you. To the right was a family room and my parents' room; to the left, there was a living room with a fireplace, and past that was the kitchen. I remember the layout well.

The home was situated beside a government housing complex populated mainly by African Americans driving Cadillacs and other large cars that emulated a certain status, and to the left side of the house lived an elderly lady; she was a retired teacher and nurse; she was friendly and loved to give my siblings and me sweet treats that she baked at the time while in Chicago two other sisters were born and my younger brother.

The family was growing, a whole house of seven, and it seemed we had a wonderful family. My parents were kind, and growing up, I remember many things, such as the four-door Rambler my father drove, and the Catholic school I used to go to just a few blocks away. I used to walk to school and there was a kid who used to bully me on my way home each day and had me terrified until my mother told me that if I allowed another boy to attack me on my way home one more day; she was going to spank me where he hit me; I took my mom seriously. Still, I knew she was using scare tactics to make me react.

I knew that if I came home again complaining that the bully attacked me, I would surely get it from my mother. As I went to bed, I was thinking about how I would stand up to that bully, so I had to create a plan of attack to get my revenge. The next day, on my way home from school, he was right on time; the bully was confidently waiting for me. I knew that if I allowed him to bully me again, I would be in trouble; I had prepared a plan the night before to get revenge. As I walked home, I could see him coming. As I got closer to home, I carried a few books in my schoolbag and held them tightly to use as a weapon to defend myself; just as the bully was within range, I could see his face, feeling satisfied that he would bully me again. The tables turned on him when he least expected. I swung my book bag, hitting him in the face. As he fell to the ground, I kicked him, and he screamed in agony. I ran away and never saw that bully again.

Another thing I remember is the restaurant my parents ran in Chicago. It was prominent, but everything seemed big when you're a child. I remember the restaurant had a makeshift home in the back in a large room with an old porcelain bathtub with ornate claw-like feet; you could see part of the drain underneath the bathtub sitting in the middle of the room with curtains around it, and I remember the pool table, it looked like the place may have been at one time a bar, my siblings and I used to play in the back room.

My two youngest sisters were always fighting. The third youngest of my sisters got the upper hand; she defended herself by biting and using her teeth as a weapon against her sister, biting her whenever they fought since they were just a year and a half apart. She'd hang on to her till she broke skin. I don't remember how that stopped, but she grew out of that stage. But I remember the beatings she received at my father's hands. I believe this was my first recollection of his abusive behavior; some days, she had her lips swollen or bleeding. I don't remember a lot about the abuse from Chicago, but who does not recognize the wounds of a bleeding child?

Ever since I was a child in my early years in Illinois, although I considered it my home, there is one thing I hated. I was born in Puerto Rico on a warm Caribbean summer day, and I wouldn't say I liked winter; walking to and from school in Chicago was problematic since they never close schools, even in the coldest of winters. I often used the excuse to stay home warm and comfy in my room, and my mother knew better. Even if I said that I was sick, she knew I was trying to stay away from the cold, and she would help me get dressed and push me out the door to brave the cruel cold walk to school.

One winter specifically, it was so cold that the schools were closed, and somehow, my mom did not get the memo; I was always looking for a reason to stay home. She knew I would cry wolf; that winter day, she woke me up and asked me to get dressed for school. I reluctantly refused to get out of bed. She pulled the covers and demanded that I get ready for school, even though I had already told her the school was closed. Despite my cries, she helped me get dressed as usual and pushed me out the door, claiming that school was not closed.

Some days, I would stay outside on the porch crying, and many days, she walked me to school, but that day was not your usual Chicago winter; the wind was fierce, and the cold was brutal. Knowing the school was closed, I sat on the porch floor, shivering and crying. Years later, my mom told me that my aunt Irma had saved my life that day; she came to my parents' home and saw me sitting on the porch, suffering from frostbite. She brought me in, and she and my mom slowly brought my body temperature back up. From that event, my mom knew we could not remain in Illinois; she feared I would die from the cruel Chicago cold.

During the summer months in Chicago, Illinois, I remember some of my after-school adventures, like the first time I met a Mexican family. Their home was close to school; they were my parent's friends, and their son was my classmate; I did not know a word in Spanish. Still, I knew the homemade tortillas were fresh, and I loved the bean burritos; one day after school, I stopped by my friend's home. All I could think about was the taste of the bean burritos.

I left school with my friend, and we went straight to the kitchen; the bean burritos were enough excitement that I was a bit late leaving while I was there. It was too dark even to know where I was, and my friend's mom called my parents to pick me up.

Another fond memory of my life in Chicago was my trips to McDonald's. I loved the food so much that I had a T-shirt with a big Mack burger on the front. It had all the ingredients from the top sesame seed bun to the bottom all in words, and I must have worn that t-shirt often to remember all the elements: two all-beef patties, special sauce, lettuce, cheese, pickles, onions on a sesame seed bun.

In my parent's home, there was only one black-and-white TV for the whole family and I remember the first color TV that my father bought, he came home with a cabinet-type TV with the usual round dials of that time to change channels, it must have cost my father a lot of money, he would sit there admiring the TV and he would brag to his friends of the lovely colors it projected my father seemed to be a different man dedicated to his family, he worked at the Kellogg's cereal company, and I remember the stories he used to share with us about the cereal packaging factory.

My father used to bring boxes of cereal since he was on the packaging line he used to drop an extra present inside the box for us to enjoy and we used to put our hands in the box to get to the gifts, we could not wait for the contents to get low enough for the presents to drop out of the bag, we were all one big happy family except for the usual arguments that all parents have from time to time, so many great memories, little did I know things were about to change.

"Child abuse is a horrific experience with lasting effects. Unfortunately, it's also a common occurrence around the world".

CHAPTER TWO
BACK TO PUERTO RICO

Encourage a child's dreams, it's a bestowed gift; but only a few manage to witness their aspirations come to fruition.

"If I wanted to feel like a girl, all I had to do was sit under the tangerine tree and dream".

In the early summer of 1971, my parents returned to Puerto Rico for the warm, never-ending summers of the Caribbean Island, where I was born. I loved the warm weather, and now we are back home.

Since my earliest recollection of home was Chicago, despite the cold, I fell in love with the windy city, and I missed it. It took me some time to get used to living in Puerto Rico, but I soon forgot about my childhood in Chicago and settled into a new life.

Another aspect that changed while in my Chicago was my father where they ran a restaurant. I do not recall the arguments or constant fights or my father's abusive behavior; everything at the time seemed normal otherwise, once an abusive parent, will always be an abusive parent.

When my parents moved to Puerto Rico with five children and another on the way, my father built a small home with the help of our new neighbors on a piece of land donated by my grandparents.

We moved into the wooden plank house with only two bedrooms, a large room for all six of us with four beds, a shared bed by two of my sisters, a crib for my brother, and a bedroom in the back for my mom and father and a large room that served as a living and family room and a dining room, and a kitchen and an outhouse behind the house on the back.

My grandfather had much land in which he had chickens, a milk cow, turkeys, a vegetable garden, fruit trees such as two types of lemons, and lime trees, pepper trees, a soursop tree, a tangerine tree, and a sugarcane field, a breadfruit tree, and a large avocado tree.

Picking fruit was much fun. I remember days when I used to sit under a tree after picking fresh fruit. I would sit under the tree enjoying a fresh natural treat. My favorite fruits were the soursop and tangerines.

Girls from the neighborhood used to sit under the tangerine tree enjoying a succulent tangerine, and that made me think that *"if I wanted to feel like a girl, all I had to do was sit under the tangerine tree and dream"*.

At that moment, I felt like a girl sitting there in a flowery tropical dress; I was a girl for that moment and wanted those moments to last forever.

My grandfather had an average Puerto Rican concrete home with three bedrooms, a dining room, a living space that shared the main room, a kitchen, two bathrooms, and a carport.

The house sat a long way from the road accessible via a long blacktop driveway to the concrete paved front of the home.

The house had a water well under the front porch, which by the 70s was no longer in use. I remember the pump on one end of the porch, which drew rainwater from under the porch.

The day we arrived at my grandparents' home. We were so excited, for the first few months, we could not communicate well with my grandparents, but since we had aunts and uncles who spoke Spanglish, we could communicate.

Everything was so new to us, and my siblings and I wasted no time looking for fun things to do.

I had never seen live chickens, lizards roaming around and so much nature to entice a young explorer's interest, I loved playing with lizards' tails, I would catch one just to hold it by the tail and laugh out loud at the lizard snapping its tail and see it run away it was so funny to see that but I never knew that was a defense mechanism to evade a predator and that the tail would grow back.

I have fond memories of playing with chickens, chasing them, and playing with ground beetles. I also had a passion for building paper planes and finding the one that flew the farthest.

I had an idea that I thought would work; the beetles used to come out at night and I would catch a few of them and carefully tie strings to their legs and the paper plane and watch as I release them to see them fly with the paper plane attached to their legs until they seem to snap the leg and escape.

There were many things to have fun with and explore, and Puerto Rico is full of interesting flora and fauna and exciting insects to play with; there were fireflies that kids used to catch in a jar to see if they could light up a room.

There were so many nocturnal insects that you could see hovering around light posts, and there was the small frog that we call Coqui, it's native to Puerto Rico and gets its name from the sound that the male makes at nightfall, (ko-kee, ko-kee) as it sings. It's a sound that all Puerto Ricans love, it's a national symbol of the island and we have many songs dedicated to the beloved Coqui.

If you are ever so lucky to find one and catch it, you can see how beautiful it is with three toes on its legs, and they are very sticky; if you catch one, they are hard to shake off, so it's best to leave them alone since they are a highly protected species, the essence and music of Puerto Rico.

Due to the surrounding mountains forming a "C" shape, the neighborhood had limited access with only two roads leading in, one to the west and one to the east.

To one side of the mountains was an open cavern with hanging vines that kids used to swing from that hovered over homes below; one day, while watching kids swing from the vines, the unexpected happened when one kid flew over a house from the vines, and it suddenly snapped.

The homes below were not so far down from the vines, and the kid landed on the concrete roof of one home.

Though he was stunned, he seemed to be okay back then. If you did not have serious injuries or were not bleeding, you could easily recover and continue playing getting hurt was not a big deal.

I used to envy kids playing around in the neighborhood; we could not venture too far away from home because my father was always on alert to our location.

My father watched us like a hawk, and the minute we were out of sight, he would come down on us like a bird of prey with anything at his disposal to inflict pain.

Before living in Puerto Rico, my father seemed well concerned and caring, but something drastically changed.

He became enraged at the slightest trigger to hit my sisters or me with anything, and his primary target was to hit us with his knuckles on the head; this is what we call in Puerto Rico a (cocotaso) I do not know how to translate that into English but believe me, it was painful.

According to a search on Google there is no translation to the word other than a description (*Cocotaso is a hard rap to the head.

Usually inflicted by an angry parent or sibling with a fist), the closest definition to this in the U.S. is a "noggin". A Noggin is an informal, slightly silly way to say "head".

This was the least severe form of punishment, but over time, this caused me a lot of hate and fear, which may have led to health issues later in life.

I often received painful strikes from my father on my head. I believe I may have had a concussion a few times. However, I never saw a doctor or received treatment for these injuries. As a result, I never fully understood the extent of the harm caused by my father. All his children, except my younger siblings, who were still babies, suffered from his abuse. One thing was certain: I hated my father.

My mother was a dedicated Christian and a loving woman; she loved her children and would give her plate to any of her children; everyone around her loved her.

A mother with a heart of gold, she was a seamstress, all women in the neighborhood, we lived in a small village called Mavito outside of the city of Dorado, Puerto Rico, even the strongest hurricane winds would be mild, and we hardly ever had wind damage.

My mom had many talents; she had a sweet voice that I loved to hear when she sang Christian music, either while cooking or doing housework or as she sat in front of her sewing machine making house gowns to sell.

Some days, she even gave a few away to less fortunate women; she was so good at making dresses she did not even carry a measuring tape with her; she could look at any woman from head to toe, fit her by eyesight, and make the dress to perfection.

She dressed many women, young and old, as well as lovely girls, including wedding dresses.

Despite all the good she did, one thing that she struggled with, as well as her children, was dealing with an abusive husband and father.

I remember my mother standing between my father and her children to stop him from beating us with his fist, kicking us around, or using whatever he had to inflict pain as he felt fit to punish his children.

Whenever my mom stood up to him, he would beat her up as well, but my mother was a fighter, and many times she stood up to him and fought as I had never seen her.

She was strong-willed and had faith that God would protect her and her children.

Her faith was more robust than anyone I knew, and she had no problems standing up to my father.

Sometimes, he was afraid of her and backed down; you cannot stop a mother when she fights to protect her children.

My mother thought about us so much, and always protected her children, but there was one thing that she never saw coming; aside from the abusive behavior of my father, there was a darker secret that even she never expected.

The child abuse from my father extended further than we ever had expected.

I felt he was more abusive toward me, and perhaps he even believed that I displeased him by being born a boy and not a girl.

However, little did he know that I always wanted to be a girl, and there may have been a more significant reason for my being born a boy.

Perhaps it was to protect me from my furthers abuse.

Everything around my father was a weapon, an instrument of pain, a hammer if he was working on the house, a garden tool if he was working outside, an automotive tool if he was working on his car, or a piece of wood.

There was nothing within his reach that he did not hesitate to use to inflict pain and suffering on his children. The more abusive he got, the more hate I had for my father.

There were moments of change in him, when he appeared to be a nice man.

I wanted those days to last forever and some days I envisioned him as a changed father, I never intended to hate him, I wanted to believe that he was a good loving man but I could never have the luxury of the model father from a TV sitcom.

Some days I would sit watching a comedy or a movie about a gentle and caring father and I would cry just as images were going through my mind as a reminder of the pain from my last beating.

There were times I remember going out with him, he seemed like a caring father such as times when we headed out to the coast to go to the beach.

My father loved to be in control of everything and he was good at planning his trips, he packed the car, took care of the food and made sure that everything was perfect and he had us all marching to one beat as he packed all of us into his car, since we were all small enough we could fit in the back seat of a four-door family car and we were off to the beach.

Then, there was the ride to Ponce, the city on the southern coast where he was born, and his mother lived.

The journey back then took hours through winding mountains and treacherous cliffs.

The beach in Ponce is crystal-clear water, I remember the centuries-old fire station that was later converted into a museum and is a historically preserved site with its horse-drawn fire wagons and the red and black paint on the building and a big water fountain on the front.

Whenever we went on a trip, my father seemed the most caring man.

I wished for those times to last and hoped that he would change; at least during those times, he seemed like a different man.

Still, when we returned home, it was the same story of abuse, pain, and misery.

He was like the monster of Dr. Jekyll and Mr. Hyde; while we were out and about the island, he was nice as he can be, but when we got home, as soon as we got out of the car.

For whatever reason he felt I found myself with another painful (cocotaso) or him hitting me with whatever he had in his hands. There was no warning.

My father filled my life with so much pain, verbal, physical, emotional and sexual abuse, and as I grew older, I became more rebellious, and I desired revenge.

I recall one day that I finally had it. I believed I could stand up to him; he was mad at me because I interrupted him while he was talking to one of his friends, and he did not like that.

I was polite, but that did not matter to him; he would verbally abuse me, hoping to intimidate me with his abusive profanity.

He demanded that I go back to where I came from. I was so mad and was not about to let him embarrass me in front of his friends; I raised my voice, and that was my mistake.

He quickly jumped to his feet, and hit me with an open hand in the face, struck me several times with his fist, and kicked me.

I ran away from him; he beat me so severely that I did not have the strength to stand up, bleeding mouth, swollen eyes, and bruises all over.

Some days, I could hear one of his friends chastise him for his abusive behavior.

He would always say that you must be tough on your children, which is how a father should teach respect to his kids.

The abuse was never reported to child protective services or the police. I doubt they would have done anything about it.

One day, my oldest sister stood up against him, and his rage reached its peak because he could not bear it whenever his children showed any signs of undermining his authoritarian rule.

He lifted my sister by her lovely long curly hair and yelled at her as she screamed in pain at the top of her lungs, which is something most Spanish men hate - being humiliated and confronted.

We were terrified that, the moment he raised a hand, we started crying and crouching into a fetal position to cover our frail bodies with hands over our heads and elbows tucked tightly into our bodies as if to protect our ribs.

Now as adults, some of us have found through X-rays of bones deformed in parts of our bodies as signs of past injuries that were never reported, the lifelong lasting signs of child abuse.

Some days, it was so severe that I would pee on myself, which infuriated him even more; it was like he did not have compassion for his children.

As I write this, I remember it like watching a horror movie reel running through my head, and I am having much trouble putting this into words without tears running down my face.

There are no words to express the pain and madness of an abused child, and my father was the embodiment of evil when he was mad;

He thought that was the way to earn his respect, but it was fear that ruled our lives and the only way out in my mind was to see him dead.

I wished many times that he would change, but there was no way you could tame a raging bull.

CHAPTER THREE
SCHOOL IS IN SESSION

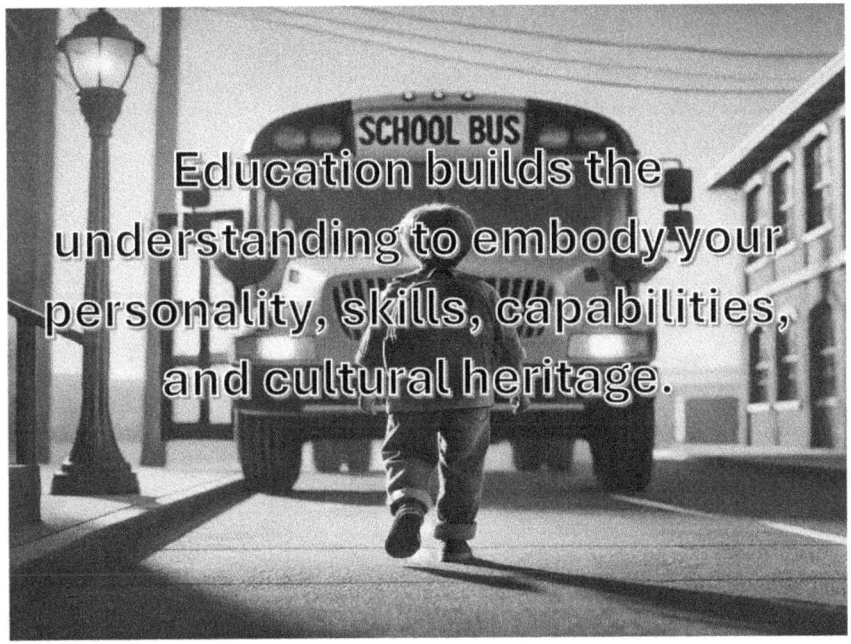

Education builds the understanding to embody your personality, skills, capabilities, and cultural heritage.

"I had to start school all over since I could not read, speak, or write in Spanish, and there were no other alternatives".

After we arrived in Puerto Rico, things drastically changed. My parents enrolled me in school shortly after we arrived on the island from Chicago. I was in the fifth grade; however, when I was enrolled in school in Puerto Rico, I did not speak Spanish. I placed in the second grade.

My first school was José Santos Alegría; *"I had to start school all over since I could not read, speak, or write in Spanish, and there were no other alternatives"*.

I had no choice; lucky for me, I landed in a room with another boy who had lived in the States and knew English and Spanish in my first year of school.

He helped me learn Spanish, and I did well in school after that, but I could never recover my lost years.

I attended my first school in Puerto Rico until I graduated from elementary to middle school just a few miles down the road to a new school, Escuela Pedro López Canino.

In the new school, I made many friends and had fresh adventures. I liked this much bigger school, and since I was well-versed in Spanish by then, I had no problem fitting in.

I was just the average Puerto Rican boy, and the new school offered a lot more ground to explore.

The number of students made it feel crowded. The school had a large cafeteria serving breakfast and lunch, so the first thing on my list was the cafeteria for breakfast.

They did a typical Puerto Rican menu consisting of vegetables, beans, meat (either pork, beef or chicken), and milk or coffee. They also had a very traditional lunch.

Yes, we occasionally engaged in food fights, but since I came from a poor background, I was taught to value food, so I rarely took part in throwing food around. I did a few times if the food fight came to me.

Usually, I would sit quietly, dodging food and trays being tossed around. However, if I became the target, I would not sit around calmly, and the few times I got into it, there were the unfortunate visits to the principal's office.

At school administrators and educators were your parents for that day and they spared no time in applying punishment to fit the crime.

They often would not spare the rod, and the sentence was rarely cruel but some teachers or administrators would get off-hand and there was little to no accountability.

If you came home that day with a note from school that you misbehaved, the punishment at home was more severe, and as abusive as my father was, that meant horror and pain.

One day I came home with a note that I verbally abused a teacher, and was disrespectful back then a verbal abuse or disrespect was anything that the adult deemed disrespectful.

When my father got the note, his first order of punishment was to slap me across the room with his open hand and beat me.

I ended up with swollen eyes, bruises and busted lips; I do not even know how I kept a beautiful smile with all my natural teeth in place.

My life endured cruel and unusual punishment. Some days, my mom would receive a note, gently slap me, and burn the message over the stovetop so that my father would not see it.

She was a loving and gentle mother, and although she believed in punishment, she never became the abusive parent my father was.

Some teachers acted like they owned you and all the children in a classroom. Children are creative and have ample energy, and when the teacher was out of the room, we all played music with our chairs.

The chairs had a wood top and seat, but the rest, including the basket for your books below the seat, had the perfect metal surface and tone for you to play music on.

If the teacher caught you red-handed or suspected that you did something wrong, it was punishment time; they made sure that they made an example of you while in the classroom and punished you by either slapping your hands with a ruler or slapping you.

Some teachers were bold enough to hit you with an open hand to the face. Others would use either a book or whatever they had to instill order, and the teacher would usually get away with it.

Then it was off to the principal's office for possible further punishment or a note to your parents; sometimes you paid the unjustified price two or three times over.

I loved school and did everything I could to excel, though my grades could have been better. I was an average B and C student, and I loved science, world history, and language, but math was my worst subject.

Reading books has always been a passion of mine and I absolutely loved immersing myself in different stories and worlds. In contrast, I would read about future technology, automotive, science, and space exploration at the library. Sometimes, I was late to a classroom as I synced myself into a book; during that time, I was in another world.

I was on safe grounds in the classroom or the library, but it was a different story when I was on school grounds.

People regarded me as a geek, but the worst part was the bullies who roamed the school grounds and targeted me.

I experienced constant bullying in school, and since my father was the worst, the school bullies merely resembled a smaller version of my father.

The abuse at home horrified me. Now, the horror continued at school, and my only refuge was the library, but sometimes, I could not go or did not make time because I wanted friendship.

Whenever I was alone, the ugliest bullies followed me, using their body mass as intimidation.

I was called ridiculous things as if I was an alien or worse. Sometimes, I would stand up to a bully when I felt I had enough.

If I had the upper hand, I would physically confront and beat up the bully, releasing my frustration on one bully at a time.

I was not a fighter by any means,

I always did what I could to stay away from a fight, but sometimes I just had to stand up and beat up someone or risk been beat up by one, two or more.

I would sometimes dream of being like superman to take revenge against my enemies, but I was skinny because I was always running, either away from my bullies or because I dreamed of being faster than the bullies.

Sometimes, my speed was all that saved me from another beating.

I was always running for my safety, but I rarely had the energy to run from the belt, fist, or whatever my father had at hand to abuse me.

Dodging bullies or belts was my life; I endured bullying, child abuse, and circumstances beyond my control that crushed my childhood dreams.

CHAPTER FOUR
THE HORROR UNFOLDING

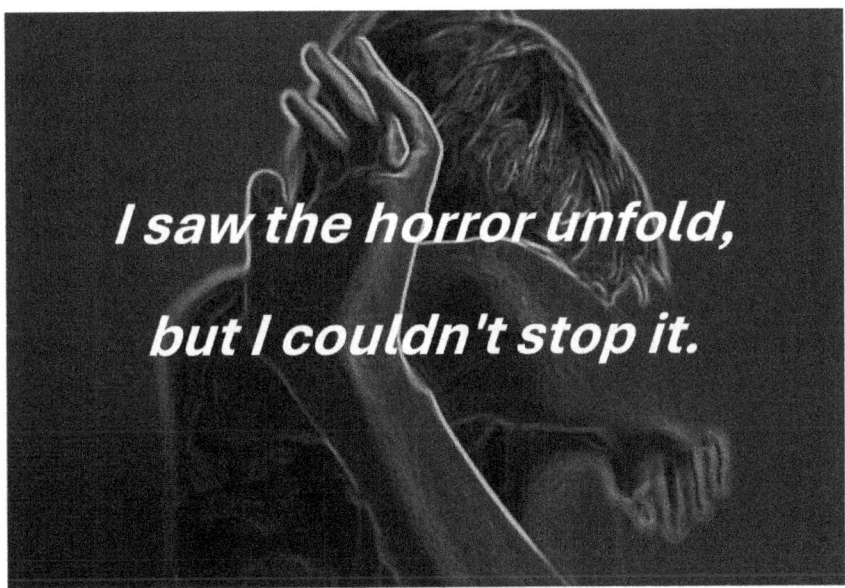

I saw the horror unfold, but I couldn't stop it.

"I cried with my hands covering my body in fear and pain at the sound of a belt striking my skin. I wanted to say I've had enough, but I was too busy screaming from the pain".

My life was like a horror movie unfolding before me in my early teens. I felt trapped, with no way out of the situation.

I raised prayers to God to change my father's behavior, I was tired of the abuse; experienced rape at ten years of age.

As a child, I believed insects had a better chance than me and felt inferior and, like living in a prison, I cannot find better analogies to describe the horror my siblings and I endured.

Sexual abuse against a child is a horrible reality of living in a sin-stricken world. A child has a special place in God's heart and anyone who harms a child is inviting God's wrath upon himself.

Pain, misery, humiliation, mental, physical, and sexual abuse filled my life. I was confused, not knowing who or what I was, and I wanted God to either make me a girl or just take my life.

The life I desired did not include living in constant fear, with no freedom of choice, and the freedom to live as I desired.

I never felt like I was a boy growing up, and I did not understand why I must live in such an abusive situation.

I loved my mother but hated my father.

Running away seemed like a way out, but I never dared to take that step because I love my mom and my siblings, but I knew that something had to change.

The 70s was the most troubling and disturbing decade of my life, and I thought it would never change. I could not imagine how it would ever change if my father did not; what would it take to make that happen?

"I cried with my hands covering my body in fear and pain at the sound of a belt striking my skin. I wanted to say I've had enough but was too busy screaming."

During the mid-70s, my parents moved to a new home closer to the city of Dorado in a new subdivision that was built by a co-op of neighbors; it was a better home made of concrete, though not much bigger than what we lived in the small village of Mavito it was a better home, and since it was closer to the coast, it had to be made of concrete to withstand possible hurricane winds. I looked at this as a change for the better.

Hopefully, my father would change his ways and treat us better, but that was just a dream witnessed only in a TV sitcom.

A new home, new neighbors, and school; by this time. I was in high school and moved to a new district in the city of Dorado.

For a short time, things felt like they were changing for the better. My father seemed to be calm. He seemed to treat us better, but that was short-lived.

The new school, Escuela Segunda Unidad de Maguayo, was great. It was further away from home, so I had to take the bus to school. I made new friends, and I loved the new school. It was larger than the last one I was in.

I felt like bullying would no longer rule my world, but as soon as I got comfortable, that soon changed, and I had the feeling of being followed.

Now I had to face bullies with bigger bodies and muscles. They wasted no time in attacking me. Gladly, by now I knew my way out was to the school library.

The library was small but full of books that I had to get my hands on; I met and built a good relationship with the librarian.

She was helpful and made me one of her assistants at the library; while I was there, if I was not reading a book, I was organizing and cataloging the books as the students turned them in; I learned where each book belonged, also assisted other students looking for reference books.

I knew all the books, the ones that interested me most where science, technology, automotive and space exploration, I read every book in series if there were more than one volume and learned of technologies of the future that are now commonplace, that was over 50 years ago and to this day I hold on to the same topics of interest.

Another subject of interest was art, and between the art room and the library, I did everything to stay away from bullies and everything to stay busy learning on my own terms.

I had no time for bullies; some days while at the library, I could see bullies like a bird of prey hunting outside the window. They were waiting for me, and the librarian knew I was trying to avoid them, some days she allowed me to stay past school so that she could take me home and did so a few times.

The last time the librarian drove me home in her new green two-door 1970s Ford Maverick with GT stripes was when I stayed late at the library.

I was afraid of my father and what he might do next time and thought that if she drove me home and explains the reason; I was late that everything would be ok.

That day, I overstayed by a couple of hours, and when I got home, my father was outside at the front door. I could tell that he was waiting for me there, and I could see in his face that he was furious.

With the anticipation of what was coming, my heart was pounding as if it was going to jump out of my chest.

I walked in through the front door, and I leaned against the wall and waited there as my mother was in the kitchen cooking. She was aware of what was happening.

The librarian drove away, and my father came back into the house; he did not immediately notice me standing at the door as he stumbled in, but as soon as he saw my mom's face, he turned around.

Mom begged him to leave me alone, but it was too late. He was like a jack in a box ready to jump into his abusive behavior, and though I tried to explain my reason for being late, he would not listen, he was ready to strike.

My father was abusive and never realized that he was creating hate in his children, and moved like a raging bull charging ready to strike.

He slapped me so hard that I flew across the room and landed right back against the wall next to the front door where he kept a sharp 36-inch-long machete he used to cut sugar cane with, and it fell right into my hands as I stood up.

As he moved closer towards me, I seized the opportunity, getting ready to slice and dice that machete was sharp enough to slice through a tomato in the air.

I was crying in pain and screamed at him. I had enough of your abuse; as he looked at me stunned, I was ready to take a stand for myself.

My adrenaline must have been high, and I ignored the pain of his hand hitting my face.

I was releasing years of hate and there was no time to cry, "*I hate you and I'm tired of your abuse, I'm going to kill you*", he replied assured of himself, "*you are a little piece of shit, you are not man enough and you don't have the balls to do it*".

He was sure I was going to coward away running and crying, but he did not realize how much anger and hate were in my innocent heart.

I thought of ways to kill my father, and I would plan it in my head, it was my mission to stop the abuse, but I was not a killer, I was a child looking to break out of the chains of child abuse by any means possible.

This moment was fast developing. I felt like it took a long time for me to deliver a stern warning to my abusive father. I was face to face with a raging bull that needed to be tamed, even if that meant his life or mine.

Like adding fuel to a fire, the hate inside of me finally flared up. He was standing just feet away from being killed by his son; thinking that because he was a grown man and a father, that he could punish his children any way he chose.

He took the bible out of context in literal terms from Proverbs 13:24 NIV - *Whoever spares the rod hates their children, but the one who loves their children is careful to discipline them.*

This in no way justifies child abuse, the keyword "careful" which abusive parents ignore over their false beliefs or ignorance.

I gripped the machete tightly to make sure it did not slip off my hands, that blade swung with so much hate that I could hear it slicing in the wind, everything at that moment was silent, I could hear a pin drop, and I had no pain, I heard no words, and though my mom was screaming at the horror unfolding before her eyes, her child with machete at hand ready to kill.

In that tense moment, my father swiftly closed the distance, his footsteps echoing on the ground. With a heightened sense of urgency, I gripped the wooden handle of the machete. As I swung it through the air, the metallic whoosh sliced through the silence. Just as my father's eyes caught sight of the machete's blade, his body recoiled, causing him to lose his balance. In a jumble of limbs, he crashed onto the hard concrete floor, the impact sending vibrations through the air while my mother screamed. He was stunned in terror.

CHAPTER FIVE
THE HIDDEN TRUTH

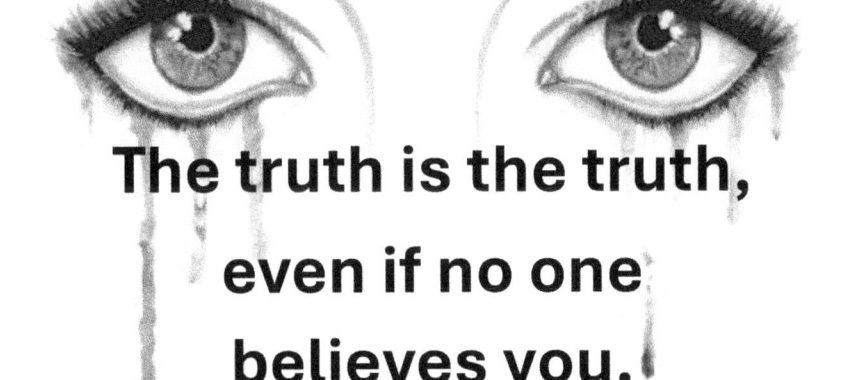

The truth is the truth, even if no one believes you.

"I was secretly raped untold times by an uncle, my father, and other boys in my neighborhood and at school".

I lived a life of fantasy and fear. Every moment he was home, I counted the bruises, both seen and unseen; there was no way out of the eye of the brutal beast. *"I was secretly raped untold times by an uncle, my father, and other boys in my neighborhood and at school"*.

I lived a double life that rarely got noticed, and when it was, I couldn't tell how painful the suffering was.

My father reacted to my sexual encounters with boys by severely punishing me with humiliating words and beatings, using his hands without mercy wherever his punishing blows landed.

He would also use his belt like a whip or kick me around like a soccer ball, while he said, *"I am going to make a man out of you."*

I suffered from gender dysphoria since I was a child. I never knew what that meant until the early 90s when I purchased my first computer and began researching, I did not know who I was, but one thing is sure: I knew I was not gay; I never identified as and never wanted that type of relationship.

My uncle, raped me many times in the bathroom at the back of my grandmother's house; he asked me not to tell anyone but the next day after that first time children and other men humiliated and called me gay in my neighborhood; he betrayed me, and I could not tell a soul.

My father found an excuse to beat us up at every opportunity. We grew up surviving horror and humiliation. We watched the clock and enjoyed freedom, at least for those few hours while he was at work.

I began dressing up in girls' clothing discretely and going out in shorts, revealing as much leg as I could, I began shaving my legs as soon as I began growing body hair so my legs were smooth and sexy, and I wanted to attract men hoping to find and escape the horror of home but that never happened and I am sure it was God's plan for my safety.

I cannot put into words the untold horror of my father's anger and abusive behavior of his children, sometimes he looked like he was a caring father while other times he looked like a madman.

His belt beating into our flesh tearing us apart, the beatings were so bad, he would start swinging that belt till we bled, and the bruises lasted a while till they healed, and no one cared to see that we were being abused by our father without compassion.

My oldest sister began dating; she had a boyfriend who lived just outside our new neighborhood.

His name was Carlos, he was nice and seemed to be friendly. He had a motorcycle and would come to visit my sister; some days, and give me a ride on his motorcycle, and other days, I remember, he would come around to play with us.

I looked up to him like a big brother I never had, and for that moment, I was happy to see someone who was caring and gentle.

That is what I saw in him, and I felt protected, at least while he was there.

I don't recall how long they dated, but I remember the day when we uncovered everything, like opening a door to a dark closet and exposing the monster inside.

My mother was a devoted Christian woman. She loved going to church; some days, we stayed home, while other days, we all jumped in my father's car and went to church as a family.

The church was a small congregation in a one room building on a mountain, and most of the people there were from the same neighborhood.

Everyone knew each other well, and there were members of my grandfather on the other side of the mountain that used to go to the same church.

My mom loved to write songs to God and would often sing at the church. She was a talented woman loved by many people, and she loved her children.

She would often make our clothes since we could not afford to go to the store and afford a lot of things, let alone clothing.

My father met Jesus through her, hoping that meeting Jesus would change the abusive behavior toward his children, but that never happened.

My father would go to church with my mom, but as soon as they left the church, he was back to his usual abusive self.

He preached the Gospel to his friends and did not waste time abusing his children; as soon as he was home, he would find a reason to continue his relentless abuse.

My oldest sister's boyfriend discovered my father's abuse when he found out that she was not a virgin.

He must have questioned her until she talked of the molestation; I can't imagine my sister's horror about sharing a dark, long-time hidden secret with her boyfriend, in fear that my father would beat her up.

Fear followed us with every step.

CHAPTER SIX
TIME TO PAY THE PRICE

When you abandon your character, you lose your freedom.

"The day of my father's arrest, I felt a great sense of relief. My siblings and I were free; we were no longer under the punishing fist of the beast".

On the day of my father's arrest, tears streamed down my face, not out of longing for him but fueled by the intense hatred within me. Despite my powerlessness to ease the anguish, suffering, and abuse he caused, his imprisonment gave me freedom.

I could now see my way clear. I don't recall the details of that day; but I remember the police arrested him at church.

I saw my father in handcuffs as he was being walked to the police car.

He had his head down and carried a sense of shame as the police finally caught him, and everyone saw his arrest, no one ever suspected that he was raping his children, he had everyone fooled.

Whatever he felt held no significance. This was the day that I waited for my entire life, and at thirteen years old, I finally saw my way clear to freedom.

My father's arrest was because of his incestuous acts of raping three of his daughters.

No one ever knew that he also raped his son on his mother's bed in Ponce and other times.

I was sexually molested and watched by him secretly as I took a shower in the outhouse, where he built a makeshift bathroom and shower set up, he could have built a bathroom inside of the house but for his pleasure instead he deliberately built an outhouse behind our home with a few discrete holes on a wall where he would watch from.

I knew he was spying through the holes to see his children as they showered or used the toilet, knowing that they were there.

That day, he took me to the city to see the sites, and that night, as we went to sleep, I lay in bed against the wall on his mother's bed while she slept in another room.

I was tired and nearly asleep when he quietly woke me. While he was touching my bottom, he asked me to pull down my underwear. I was terrified of him and in fear of being beaten so I complied.

I was scared, and he took advantage of me, already confused, raped, horrified, and disgusted by his next request.

I thought that my father might have been gay at one time in his life when asked me to turn around and return the favor.

I was so disgusted that I could not even get hard to proceed with his request. He fondled me, but I could not do it.

He got mad but quietly told me not to tell my mother what had just happened. I could not sleep that day.

"The day of my father's arrest, I felt a great sense of relief. My siblings and I were free" we were no longer under the punishing fist of the beast".

No one can ever understand what it's like to live your childhood in such an abusive situation with a parent who ruled with an iron fist.

A father who used his children as he saw fit, who physically tortured and took away a sense of security from his children. A father who raped and carried on like it was a normal family home.

I was slowly developing a killer mentality; I can't remember how many times I dreamed of the best way to kill my father.

The day I nearly killed him with a machete cutting though his fat hairy belly, I wished it had come through, and I would find freedom earlier in life; even after my father fell in prison, I wanted to kill him.

I had so much hate in my heart because his brutal abuse poisoned me.

He is now dead, but the horror of those memories remained with me, and this is the only way that I can lay it all to rest.

As painful as this is, the truth must be told.

Shortly after my father's arrest, my mother's financial situation couldn't cover the mortgage on our home in the new neighborhood.

She sold the house at a cheap price, and purchased a manufactured home, and had it built on the same land my grandparents gave her behind their home in Mavito.

They had taken apart the first home we lived in, piece by piece and used the wood for other projects, which I was happy to hear since we suffered so much under my father's hands in that house.

It took about a month to build the new home, and my mom moved with her six children to a home with three bedrooms, and for the first time a bathroom with a flushable toilet and a shower, a kitchen and dining room, a living room, and a small porch out front.

My brother and I shared one bedroom, my sisters all shared the larger room, and my mom had her bedroom; we finally lived in peace except for the occasional sibling rivalry over children's dumb reasons to fight, but we were free of abuse.

My mom laid the law sometimes, but her punishment was mild in comparison, and she never treated us to fear her, she was kind and caring, living with my mom was great.

I had all the freedom a child could have since I was the second oldest and a male it was my time to step up to the plate.

Constant fear characterized my childhood, as my father cared only for his satisfaction if he had the upper hand.

Now that I am free and no longer afraid of his abuse, he was far out of reach, and I wish he had stayed there for the rest of his life; history has a cruel way of finding its way back.

CHAPTER SEVEN
THE MAN OF THE HOUSE

I wiped away my sorrows and walked through the door to freedom.

"After my father's arrest, we lived off food stamps and whatever we could harvest from my grandfather's garden".

My mom divorced my father while he was in prison, and was ready to move back to her land in Mavito. I was now in my mid-teens and in the eighth grade in the city of Maguayo when we returned to Mavito, which meant that I had to return to the school I left before.

Returning to that school was not an option for me, I knew some of my old bullies were still there, and after having found a new sense of freedom, I did not want to land back in the clutches of bullies, but I loved school, however, as long as I stick to my plan to spend my time in the library while everyone else played in the schoolyard; I was safe, sadly plans drastically changed once again.

"The most important door of your life is the door to freedom"

Back in Mavito, I looked forward to moving on with my life. My progress was clear, and my desire to attend art school was strong.

I always looked for ways to improve my work and impress my teachers, while at the art class, I met a cute young teacher. I had a secret crush on her; she was my art teacher, and I was just a boy growing up and discovering myself.

One day, she wanted to test my skills and asked me if I could draw her face. I was always shy and could not tell her I liked her, and perhaps this was my opportunity.

I grabbed my sketch pad and pencil and drew.

It took me a few minutes but seemed like hours to pencil draw her beautiful face, and once completed, I showed her my drawing, and she loved it.

Several teachers were interested in helping me start my career in art, and this was my opportunity to show what I can do.

I presented her with the drawing, and she was delighted at how well I portrayed her lovely face on paper and said that she was going to connect me with a Puerto Rican artist named Ali from the city of Dorado who studied his art in Italy.

Things were turning around for me, I was ready for a career, this was going to open the doors for me and hopefully see my dreams come true and I no longer had an abusive father to hold me back, but the move back to Mavito changed things for me once more.

I needed a job to help my mom and my younger siblings. For the next few years, I became like a father, to the youngest of my sisters and brother.

My teacher helped me get a job in the city of Dorado as an artist, designing and painting murals on government apartments.

The project lasted six months, and during that time, I earned a decent income and got paid my salary plus a per diem for meals and transportation expenses.

I kept the smaller check, which was enough for my expenses, and gave the larger check to my mom to feed my siblings, once the job ended I was back on the hunt to employment.

My last job in Puerto Rico was at a seafood restaurant in the city of Cataño, next to San Juan. From where the restaurant was located, I could see the east walls of the old Spanish fort San Cristobal del Morro.

I loved cooking, and I wanted to be a chef and loved working in the kitchen.

I worked there for a few months making shrimp with "tostones," a fried food staple made with green plantains and seasoned with fresh garlic and breaded shrimp, and everyone loved the food.

On the fourth of July, at the fort, they used to fire the cannons, and you could hear it from the restaurant; it was loud, but it was a site that everyone eating there enjoyed, the pride of Puerto Rico.

That was my last job in Puerto Rico; and it was hard to find a new job. I felt frustrated because I didn't know how I would help my mom support my four younger siblings.

"After my father's arrest, we lived off food stamps and whatever we could harvest from my grandfather's garden." Things were not easy, but at least we were well-fed, cared for and no longer abused.

I loved riding my bike around the island on my time off. I was out exploring the city of Toa Baja, close to my neighborhood, and as I walked, I saw something that caught my attention in a store window.

I turned around and saw a plastic model of a 1931 Rolls Royce Phantom; I did not know what I was getting into; but I bought the car and headed back home.

That first model awoke in me a passion for cars, I had a collection of models, including antique cars, a model rocket and model ship of the Mayflower and a model of the USS Constitution, plus a model of a Freightliner cab-over truck with a Bird's-eye frozen vegetable trailer and a 70s Mustang with two jet skis on a trailer, about 30 models in all.

The authorities sent my father to one of Puerto Rico's toughest prisons, Oso Blanco (White Bear), in the city of Rio Piedras.

I hated him so much that I never thought I would see him again. I wished for him to root in prison the rest of his life for all the pain he caused his children and the trauma of being abused in so many horrible ways.

After my father left prison, he reemerged into existence. It looked like he was now a changed man, slimmer and clean.

Though I hated him, he was still my father, at least I said hello to him. He came to say goodbye; and was leaving Puerto Rico to live in Atlanta, Georgia; he had a job lined up, and I was glad he was leaving.

My mother did not want a relationship with the man that abused her children.

I had so much fun exploring Puerto Rico on my bike and go to any city or place I wanted to; riding my bike all day from sunrise to sunset as far away as the city of San Juan on the east coast or to the city of Arecibo on the west coast.

I spent a lot of time at Dorado Beach; I knew a lot of places and frequently traveled to the northern coast of the island and would often return home late. My mother was always worried, but I was ok. I had a few scary situations but always stayed away from danger.

When I was not on my bike I was hitch hiking the island and I could go to further out places, during those days it seemed like a safe thing to do, the last time I hitchhiked could have been a catastrophic mistake and my name could have ended a statistic on a newspaper headline.

I was hitchhiking and had already taken two short trips to wherever the ride took me, and I would take another ride, I was headed to the city of Dorado. The third ride was with an old man in his late 40s or early 50s, he seemed like a nice guy when he stopped to give me a ride to my destination.

I jumped in the front seat since he popped open the passenger door and I closed the door, as soon as he started to drive he began asking questions and I casually and politely answered his questions which seemed like normal conversation, then things got weird.

The man started to touch himself and continued asking questions and then he unzipped his pants and exposed himself to me asking if I liked men, I got scared and my heart began racing, he was masturbating himself and said that he was going home and wanted me to come with him.

I did not know what to do but I know I needed a way out but I could not do that while he was speeding down the road.

There was light traffic but there was plenty of cars around with two cars leading him just as a traffic light was changing he had to stop, thanks God, I thought, this was my way out.

Before he could reach out to me when he saw my hands on the door handle to open it and jump out I managed to get away from him and I ran back as fast as I could, my heart was pounding hard at the sight of what could have happened to me and that was the last time I hitchhiked.

My friends and neighbors began to smoke, and I took up smoking Virginia Slims, the only cigarette with a woman's name, and as I smoked, I felt like a woman.

I would go out at night with other teens in my neighborhood and go to bars; back then, no one checked our ID.

We could go to a store and buy beer and liquor; Bacardi 100 was the strongest rum. The oldest one in the group would buy a bottle and we sat in a circle to pass it around and see who would pass out drunk first until it was all gone.

We stole chicken to make soup to sober up, and then later, some of my friends got into marijuana. This was a new thing, and I loved the rush it used to give me.

I got into sexual encounters with other boys, and they called me the gay next door. I didn't like being called gay. But I didn't know what else described me. There had to be something else.

I lived the best years of my teenage years, between 15 to 18 years of age.

I did what I wanted to without my abusive father; no one ever bullied me again, and my father was no longer in control of my life.

I was still without a job, and some of my friends also had no job, so there were so many opportunities to get into mischief.

Some of my friends looked to robbing stores and stealing cars, while others got into drugs like cocaine and other heavy drugs.

I was in my room when the teenager next door came over to my mom's house one day.

Back then, you could leave your front door wide open, and no one dared mess with your property, so leaving the door open or unlocked was common.

He walked in and came to my room where I was, and he showed me a red vial. He said that it was going to make me feel good.

With a syringe in his possession, he was prepared to insert the needle into the container to administer the injection to me.

I did not know what that was, but I knew in my mind that it was not safe, and I didn't want that, I told him that if he was still my friend, to take that thing away from me and get out of my house.

That was the last time I saw him; he ended up deep in drug abuse and prostitution and years later while I was already in Atlanta, I heard through other sources that he ended his life with an overdose.

I am happy to have left Puerto Rico when I did, that saved my life, but now my life was about to take a turn in another direction.

CHAPTER EIGHT
AN UNEXPECTED JOURNEY

Dreams find discovery in the unknown.

"I enjoyed reading books, and remembered an article I read about electric cars, and I had an idea".

My family gradually moved from Dorado, Puerto Rico, to Atlanta, Georgia, with each member leaving at different times.

After my father's release from prison, he started the move, followed by my oldest sister, and then the rest of us. I followed her, then my mom and the rest of my siblings.

My oldest sister moved to Atlanta, Georgia, in the early spring of 1980; and stayed with one of my father's sisters, who helped her move to Atlanta, one of the closest relatives of my father's family.

She said there was more money and jobs in Atlanta, and she seemed happy, but I did not want to be close to my father; however, being without a job at any age once you get used to making money is difficult.

Being unemployed is difficult, regardless of age. It becomes even harder when you're accustomed to earning money. In Puerto Rico, finding a new job was challenging. The money I had was insufficient. After some time, my father learned about my unemployment.

This was about a couple of years after his release from prison and his move to Atlanta.

I loved Puerto Rico and wanted to stay there. I had a good relationship with my grandfather, and he loved his grandson so much that when he heard I was planning to move to Atlanta, he offered me incentives to stay.

He knew I loved working on cars. In the past, I worked with my friends to fix up old cars and talked a lot about becoming a mechanic.

I enjoyed doing bodywork, hammering out dents on rusted old cars, and sometimes bought body filler and spray painted the pieces I fixed; I was good at figuring things out independently.

Some kids in my neighborhood had go-karts, and I wanted one, but we were poor, and could not afford one.

I drove a friend's go-kart, and I noticed how simple it was. *"I enjoyed reading books, and remembered an article I read about electric cars, and I had an idea"*.

Among my findings, I stumbled upon an old washing machine with a motor, I had an Idea to make an electric go-kart and be the first to build one.

I was ready to move forward and start building. I enjoyed having big ideas, and once I was determined, all I had to do was start implementing my plans.

My mom had recently purchased a new washing machine a model that had a head of rollers on the top of the deck that you put your clothes through after they were cleaned, and squeeze the clothes dry enough so that when you hang them on the line, they dry faster and the old washing machine was still sitting around rusting away.

I knew the motor was still working. Finding spare parts to complete my project was not a problem.

I had a passion for disassembling electronics and would happily grab a screwdriver to explore their inner workings. My mom punished me for taking things apart many times, but I was skilled at fixing them.

I found spare wheels from an old wheelbarrow, two more from hand truck for the front, built a sturdy wooden frame and began putting all my parts together.

I built my go-kart in just a few days using a washing machine motor and a bicycle drive chain.

With a large supply of junk cars, there was no problem finding a car battery, but I was missing one important part.

I could not use the car battery for my go-kart. I did not know that I needed a power inverter. If I had realized it earlier, I could have been the first in my neighborhood to build an electric go-kart.

Not having my father around allowed me to explore my mind like any child my age. I had so many ideas, but because my plans to further educate myself were taken away by circumstances of the past, I had no one to encourage me to complete my education.

I could have been an artist, a scientist, or an engineer. I had the determination and desire to succeed, but my wings were clipped during my early years growing up under the shadow of an abusive father.

The worst part was that I disliked the name of the man I hated so much, I was not the second or third in a generation of men that carried the family name, and I wanted to change it but I lacked the knowledge of how to change my name.

I had an active imagination, explored, and dared to learn at every turn, I was always reading books to supplement my education.

My mom purchased an encyclopedia Britanica of about 30 volumes and made a sacrifice that only a loving mother made for her children.

I read every book cover to cover and did not want the lack of school to stop me from learning because, at a young age.

I learned that some of the greatest minds were made not because of higher education but because of the enduring will to learn despite the lack of a formal education because they believed in a cause and stuck to their determination and became names talked about in history books.

CHAPTER NINE
A SECOND CHANCE

"I didn't think that I would ever find a way to forgive my father, let alone live with him again. I believed that if my father had changed, he deserved a second chance".

In Puerto Rico, I struggled with unemployment and had no prospects for a good job. My father sent a letter to my mom offering to send me a one-way trip to Atlanta and that he already had a job waiting for me that paid well.

In the early 80s, pay was not as ideal as today, but it was an improvement for me. I intended to work in Atlanta for two years, send money to my mom, and then go back to Puerto Rico.

"I didn't think that I would ever find a way to forgive my father, let alone live with him again. I believed that if my father had changed, he deserved a second chance."

The day I left Puerto Rico for Atlanta, I cried so much. It was Friday, July 10, 1981. I loved the island so much; I knew the island so well, at least the northern coast, as I traveled nearly the entire northern coast on a bike from east to west.

I loved the beach and the Caribbean sun. Living on the island was a paradise, and I had a tough time departing the land that I loved so much; even though I lived only ten years, I felt like I was there my whole life, and my heart was being torn apart as I realized the airplane was taking off for the last time.

I did not know whether I would ever return or make Atlanta my home.

As the airplane lifted off the ground, I looked out the window and began singing a song titled "En mi Viejo San Juan" (In my Old San Juan). Composed by Noel Estrada in 1942, the song has become an anthem of Puerto Rico.

The higher the airplane lifted off the ground, the more I could see the island slowly vanish from view.

I sang that song and cried as I drifted off to sleep. When I woke up, I watched as the airplane landed at the Atlanta Hartsfield International Airport, as it was known back then.

I realized it was a bigger airport. In contrast, the airport in Puerto Rico only had one hangar, but the Atlanta airport was a world on its own.

Once I arrived at the airport and took the train to the baggage claim for my bags, there he was.

My father was waiting for me with an entourage of family members, two of my cousins and his sister. I had not seen her in a long time since the last time I saw her in Puerto Rico.

The drive from Atlanta to Buckhead at Palmour Court Apartments, my first home with my family, felt cozy despite its size.

My first year in Atlanta was tough, unfamiliar surroundings, no bike, no direction.

I weighed 128 pounds when I came from Puerto Rico. After a year, my weight increased to 165 pounds because of my inactive lifestyle. I had no choice, which made me feel bad about myself. My lack of knowledge of my surroundings made it difficult for me to freely move around.

During the two years I lived with him in my aunt's apartment, I simply ate, sat, and watched TV. Despite no longer having the same feelings for him, I believed I could trust him because he seemed different.

It felt like my father was too good to be true - his laughter, smile, and meticulous approach to our public engagement and time at my aunt's apartment.

Some days, I could see the abuse reflecting from him like images of the horror I endured under his relentless abuse back in Puerto Rico. I struggled to believe that this man genuinely changed after being in prison for five years.

I wanted to pull the curtains off him, but something was wrong.

Was it my imagination playing these images as a black-and-white film running through my memory? How can I purge these memories and learn to trust him?

My father desired to move out, but not by himself. In his quest for a roommate, he expressed his wish to find a suitable candidate.

I knew he was searching, but I did not know he wanted me to be his roommate until the day he asked me to move in with him. Was this his way of taking charge?

He had everything well calculated and knew what he was doing, but I was still the innocent Puerto Rican boy living in Atlanta and had little choice.

Reluctantly, I made the move with him; I loved living with my aunt and my two cousins, and now that has changed.

We used to play a lot together on the classic version of Atari that came out in the early 80s with individual game cartridges.

We have advanced beyond the era when games had pre-installed features and limited options. Living with my cousins was a lot of fun.

The day I moved in with my father was on a Saturday morning. I felt a mix of emotions and excitement simultaneously.

It was a one-bedroom with a bathroom, kitchen, and a small dining room.

The bedroom had enough space for two double beds and walking space on each side.

He took the window side, and I took the side by the door. I had my closet space, and he had his.

Everything seemed to go smoothly for a while. When I was home, I had the freedom to play with my cousins. Sometimes, I would stay up late watching The Twilight Zone and The Outer Limits and then wake up on the couch.

I was feeling comfortable, but things changed about six months after moving in with my father; it was now late 1982 when I noticed the changes.

My early life in Atlanta was met with a whirlwind of change and personal growth, from an innocent young man to a grown, independent man and earn my respect.

CHAPTER TEN
THE WAKE-UP CALL

Remain alert everything is not always what it seems to be!

"I was tired, and I slowly woke up. I did not want him to think that he could control and manipulate me as he did when I was a child."

I noticed changes in my father's behavior; somehow, I wanted to believe that it was all in my mind, but I could not help noticing the progression in his controlling behavior.

Initially, I worked at an Italian restaurant in Perimeter Mall, but it was short-lived. I love cooking but could not do well enough to satisfy a demanding Italian chef.

My father got me a job in a textile company called Atlanta Bias, where he worked in the city of Chamblee, Georgia. I spent a few years working there, but things were changing.

My paycheck was not mine to decide. It was unfortunate that I did not have a bank account to rely on.

From that point on, he took control of my finances. I couldn't spend my own money without his permission.

During tax season, he made decisions based on his money and mine. I had to eat what he cooked. His cooking left much to be desired, and on top of that, I had to constantly seek his approval for each action I took, including notifying him of my intended destination and providing him with a thorough update of my whereabouts.

"I was tired, and I slowly woke up. I did not want him to think that he could control and manipulate me as he did when I was a child."

I had to take a stand. I took a day off work to go to the bank and open my first checking and savings account. Despite being unaware of my earnings, my father still sought control.

During the tax season in 1982, he decided he wanted to buy a car, and was making plans once more with my money and his.

The difference now was that he had to make me aware of his plans, since he did not have full control of my money.

When he needed money, he had to ask me, and whenever we went out to eat or watch a movie, he cunningly made me pay for it.

It was time to act and assert myself.

One of my cousins had purchased an Australian moped brand named Puch.

I rode it a few times and fell in love with it. I had no money for a car, so I got an affordable moped with no license required.

I did not know how to prepare my taxes, so I had to depend on my father to go to a tax office to do my taxes.

With knowledge of my earnings, approximately $450, he had already computed that, when combined with his, it would cover a down payment on a car.

This was the strategy that he had devised for the situation at hand. I was ready to take a stance and assert myself. I skipped work when my tax check arrived.

I already looked at a little red Puch moped with a two-speed transmission and was ready to buy it with money at hand.

It was cute and fast, and I loved it; the salesperson at the shop had previously advised me he could help me cash my income tax check to buy the moped. Upon receiving my check, I went to the dealer and purchased my moped.

The same day I bought my moped was the last day I lived with my father. Once I arrived at my new apartment, I carefully draped a canvas cover over the shiny new moped I had just bought. This moped brought me immense joy and the sense of freedom that I had been longing for.

I had planned to surprise my father and show him I could make my own decisions. He arrived home from work at 1:30 pm after working half a day on Saturday, and I was ready for him.

I sat at the edge of my bed when he walked into the room, and he appeared tired but with a big smile on his face.

His commitment was to cover the car's initial payment. He planned to come home, take our money, and buy the car that he claimed was for both of us.

He stood on one side of his bed, and I stood on the other side, both ready for something to go wrong. Suddenly, the furious bull woke up and was prepared to charge.

He stood just feet away from me and was sure he had the money for the car. He knew I received my income tax and asked me to go with him to the dealer to buy the car.

I replied, expressing my inability to pay, and he demanded an explanation for what had occurred. Didn't you receive your tax check? I told him I received my check, but I decided to buy a moped, and I wanted to show it to him, which was sitting outside covered.

He responded to me like the fiery loudmouth he was. "You are not man enough to make that decision." Despite everything, I am here near the man I longed to trust.

I was stunned, but not so much. This is what I expected of him. I was waiting for him and suddenly I came to realize he was untrustworthy.

My dad tried to block my exit running after me out of the room but, I had enough energy to outrun him as he was coming around the bed to where I stood, I quickly reacted, and ran out the door, my adrenaline was high, and I was running for my safety and he was trying to keep up.

He was no longer fast as he was when I was a child, and he showed signs of fatigue keeping up with me. I made it to my moped, sitting outside the door in the parking lot.

I did not know how I could do it that fast, but I removed the cover, unlocked it, kick-started the engine, and got away from my father.

He was catching his breath, which allowed me enough time to reach my aunt's apartment.

Fear consumed me on that day. She helped me calm down and went to my father's apartment to talk to him. I do not know exactly what they discussed, but I am certain it was intense.

About an hour later my aunt came back from my father's apartment, she told me I was not going back to living with him. She was aware of his abuse and vowed to protect me.

That was the last time I lived with my father because he proved that he never changed. Under a cloak of obscurity, he was still an abusive father.

I lived with my aunt and my cousins for a few months, and around December 1983, I met a Dominican woman who lived just a few units down from my aunt's apartment.

Life changed rapidly during my initial three years in Atlanta. I never expected such a significant shift. While I expected things to get better, I had to be patient. God did not ignore my prayers.

I did not come to Atlanta to be abused by my father and relive what happened back in my land of birth, the land of Mi Viejo, San Juan.

CHAPTER ELEVEN
ON MY OWN

In search of a new journey.

"While living together, I tried to keep my dual identity
a secret, but she eventually caught on."

Shortly after moving back in with my aunt, I tried to build a relationship with my father once more with my aunt's help.

She had my father under advice and would not allow him to touch me; however, with his help, I learned to drive on a 1975 Chevrolet Caprice Classic wagon through the narrow streets of Buckhead,

Shortly thereafter I bought my first car, a silver 1978 Chevrolet Chevette hatchback with a four-speed manual transmission which my dad showed me how to drive and helped me get my first driver's license.

In the early 80s in the state of Georgia there were no Spanish translations to the driver's manual or the test so I had to do my best to learn the manual, the day of the test I prepared a small piece of paper stuffed inside a pen that I brought with me with questions and answers.

I hid it inside the cylinder of the pen but I was scared that I would be caught cheating but I passed the test at 85% without it and I was proud of myself with a new driver's license at hand.

Finally, I had a reliable car and was free from my father's control. I had no desire to return and live with him. Was this the end of our relationship?

Was meeting her the start of a wonderful friendship, love, or simply a means to escape?

While washing my car, I listened to Michael Jackson's music in the beginning and later switched to Puerto Rican music. When she came outside, she heard familiar music.

I had seen her before, but I did not know she spoke Spanish. When she heard me playing salsa music, she came out onto the porch and asked me where I was from.

Our conversation began at that moment.

Over time, our friendship grew stronger, and we became great friends. I was fifteen years younger than her, but we fell in love.

I had never had a real relationship before and never intended to fall in love, but it happened. Shortly after two months, I moved in with her, and my life changed overnight, at last, I experienced true masculinity.

Once I moved and got settled, I had a room across the hall from her. We could see each other sitting in bed through the open doors. I never confessed my feelings of wanting to be a woman.

Shortly after I moved in, we began sleeping together. I did what I could to live as a man with her and love her; age was not a barrier for love.

I had girlfriends in Puerto Rico, but nothing serious. When I tried dating girls from my hometown, we ended breaking up.

Some girls assumed I was gay because I did not want to have sex and reveal that I was wearing women's underwear.

"While living together, I tried to keep my dual identity a secret, but she eventually caught on."

With her nursing background and understanding of psychology, she was adept at reading people's emotions.

One day, as I sat in bed with her, she asked me if I was all right since she found a box in my room that I was hiding with women's lingerie.

Embarrassment and worry consumed me, fearing that she would kick me out and that this would damage our relationship.

I revealed to her my gender identity and desire to undergo surgery. She understood and listened attentively.

I was worried our friendship would be ruined, but she understood. We didn't sleep together after that, but we stayed in adjacent rooms.

I lived with her for nearly a year. During that time, I gave my father another chance to have a relationship with his son.

I gave my father untold opportunities; I used to give him a ride to work. He had his own car, but he was taking advantage of a free ride with me to work.

My father's newest roommate was my uncle, who divorced his wife, my father's youngest sister. They both rode with me to work and back for a while.

He had a hold on me, always prying into my relationship and making demands for money and rides, offering no support or repayment.

Neither he nor my uncle offered to help with gas money or when my car broke down. I had a plan to make them both pay.

I chauffeured my father and uncle, always sitting in the back seat. On my way to work one day, I stopped at a gas station at the pump. I sat, waiting to hear their response.

As the first speaker, my father impatiently asked, "what are you waiting for?" We are going to be late for work.

I took advantage of the situation to demonstrate that I am not afraid to express my thoughts. In a sarcastic tone, I informed my father that my car requires gas and unfortunately, I do not have the money. Considering that we all travel together, and the car does not run on water, it's your turn to pay.

I could hear my father speaking through clenched teeth, clearly angry. It was clear he disliked my response.

He asked me if I was giving all my money to my girlfriend, and I told him that what I did with my money was not his business.

Both my dad and uncle were shocked, but my uncle recognized I was standing up for myself.

They reluctantly gave me ten dollars each, and I used it to fill up my tank and have money left over for lunch.

Standing up to my father for the first time felt satisfying, and I was no longer afraid of him, and he could no longer control or beat me.

In the summer of 1983, my roommate and I moved to Sandy Springs, Georgia. We settled in an apartment community called The Southern Trace, which was a two-bedroom townhome about thirty minutes away.

The lower level had a large living room with a fireplace, a guest bathroom, a dining room, and a kitchen with ample cabinet space, and upstairs, there was a bathroom and two bedrooms on either side.

I forgot about living with my father and did not miss him. We rarely talked, and I felt like he was not my father anymore.

My father was never the same after I stood up to him. He realized I had grown confident and no longer feared him.

It took courage for me to confront him and demand respect. From then on, he could not manipulate, abuse, or take advantage of me financially.

My father had more than his fair share of a second, third, and fourth opportunity to be the father he never was to his children.

Over the preceding years, we all tried working with him, but he always showed signs of attempted manipulation.

He reached out to me multiple times via phone, by then we all had mobile phones, and our communication was good. We had a mutual respect; however, the father-and-son bond had faded away.

The last time we spoke, he was trying to make amends by joining The Church of Jesus Christ of Latter-day Saints and dedicating himself to Jesus. He invited me to go, but I declined because it was too far away.

Whether he was faking or truly caring, I could not rely on the man I hated and wanted no association with.

CHAPTER TWELVE
I DECLARE YOU MAN AND WIFE

She came into my life and never left.

*"I never knew that I could fall in love again. in early 1992
she walked into my life, and we never stepped apart".*

Life in Sandy Springs was good, I had several jobs after I left the textile company where I worked alongside my father.

I desired to distance myself from him and his unpredictable and harmful conduct; My life was flourishing from all perspectives. I had money, a bank account, a car, and more than I ever had.

Despite being single, I did not desire a family because of my gender issues. My circle of friends had expanded. Happiness filled me as I had all I desired.

I attended a Presbyterian church in the city of Marietta with close friends. One of my friends was a woman from South America married to a Japanese man. Our acquaintance lasted a few years.

She called me one day to say that she met a young, beautiful Japanese woman who she spoke to about me and asked if I was open to meeting her.

I was sitting at home with a broken left leg from a car accident on February 14 of 1992, despite my broken leg, I agreed to meet her. The young Japanese woman came to meet me in Sandy Springs.

"I never knew that I could fall in love again. In June 1992 she walked into my life, and we never stepped apart."

Once my leg healed and I was back on my feet and back to work, I moved to Marietta, GA to a single-room apartment, two months after we met, we lived together. My life underwent another significant change overnight.

We lived in that tiny apartment for half a year. Near the end of the lease, one morning she woke up early even though she was tired from working late shifts at a Japanese restaurant nearby.

I fell in love with her as I sat there, captivated by her sweet and delicate nature. Positioned at the same height as the counter, I sat on a bar stool so that we could maintain eye contact. Out of the blue, she gazed at me and said, "Will you marry me?"

In December, right before our lease ended, I enthusiastically stood up, hugged her, and said yes.

We were all set to move to a home in Smyrna, Georgia, in January 1993.

While planning our future together, I quickly seized the opportunity to call my supervisor and take the day off. We got married at the Cobb County Superior Court in Marietta, GA on January 11, 1993.

After we married and moved to Smyrna, we were so happy together, we had plans to have a family; and worked hard to make it happen, and just when we thought she could not have children, it happened.

She was expecting our first child, and we were happy since she was nearly in her mid-30s. This was our only opportunity to have a child, as we believed. We went to Kennestone Hospital for a sonogram, and the doctor showed us the child in the womb, well-developed and healthy. It's a girl said the doctor.

We drove home silently that day, both feeling disappointed that it was not a boy and sharing the same thoughts. In a bold move, she was the one to break the silence, and said, I am sorry it is not a boy.

We hugged and cried. Then, it hit us. This might be our only child. We cherished and loved her. Finally, in June 1994, she was born.

Inspired by the movie Dr. Zhivago from 1965, based on a romance novel, my wife chose the name Katiya, and dreamed of someday giving the name to her daughter, a dream come true.

She was expecting our second child a year and a half later. When we wanted to reveal the gender, we went to Saint Joseph Hospital. The doctors wanted to do an amniotic fluid test because she was 35 and considered older, just to ensure the baby's health.

A week before the amniotic fluid test, I had a dream.

In my dream, I saw myself outside in darkness walking towards a closed door. Despite the darkness, I could perceive the door's illuminated outline.

Upon opening the door, I discovered a dimly lit room with a solitary chair in the center. Despite my confusion about being there, I felt a gentle force urging me to take a seat.

There was nobody around to be seen. I sat in that chair, and I could hear my heart gently beating in a calming musical rhythm. With each passing moment of time, the longer I waited, the more I questioned my reason for being there.

The room suddenly brightened, vanishing everything in a bright light. A deep male voice echoed, proclaiming, "You are going to bear a son and his name will be Samuel."

I woke up crying and dropped to my knees and said a prayer because I knew that was the voice of God.

He had a gift for me, and I knew this was real; I held onto that dream and only shared it with my wife and no one else; it was a secret only revealed for me and her.

The next morning, I told her about my dream, but she did not believe it and thought it was just a fantasy. I did not require any validation or approval from others. I only cared about my son's health.

The day of the procedure arrived and the doctor assisted my wife onto the bed, and I witnessed a long needle being inserted into the womb to extract the amniotic liquid.

I was worried because I had never witnessed such long needles before, however; he used a monitor to guide the needle with precision and successfully collected the fluid sample he needed from the womb.

It felt like an eternity before the doctor returned with the test results. Suddenly, he reappeared and showed us the DNA test results of the parents by placing a Xray-like sheet on the lighted board.

I wanted him to confirm that the child is healthy, as I believed deep in my heart that God had promised me a son. I stood beside him, and he shook my hand tightly, and said, "Congratulations!" you are going to be the father of a healthy son.

My wife and I broke down in tears as she lay in that bed. We drove home from the hospital happy; our family was now a family of four.

My son was born on June 1996 just as the Atlanta Olympic Games were unfolding on TV across the world; we were so happy and lived in

Smyrna, Georgia, in a rental home three years before we bought a home a short distance away in Powder Springs GA.

Though I was happy during our marriage, I did not feel like my life as a married man was what I wanted. We fell in love, and things developed so fast that I lost track of time.

Deep inside, I still had gender issues I needed to address, and she needed to know the truth; there were signs through our marriage of my gender issues.

I confessed to her about my issues, which was painful but necessary. Through online research, I realized I am a transgender woman, and the signs were obvious.

I collected enough information to begin my transition, and she was aware of it. We had stopped being intimate six years before I came out. My children also knew about my gender issues and were gradually learning to accept and love their father, although things had changed.

Thirty years after our marriage, I came out in late September 2021 at 59, and today, I am back on my own. I am still married to the Japanese woman I fell in love with.

My children still call me "Papi" or father in Spanish. I stay in touch with her and my children and I live just fifteen minutes from the home we shared for so long.

I changed my legal first name from Tomas to Tamara on December 30, 2021. At the sound of the gavel that day, the female judge presiding over the case dropped the gavel. Over time, I changed my name to all my legal documents. The name Tomas, which has been passed down in my family, serves as a reminder of the abuse I suffered from my father. I didn't want the name because it reminded me of painful childhood memories.

CHAPTER THIRTEEN
FORGIVENESS IS FREEDOM

"I forgive my father, but this does not mean that I accepted his behavior or that I would ever trust him again".

The outcome of life is perpetually unpredictable and full of uncertainty. In thirteen chapters, I have documented the painful truth of my life as a child who experienced abuse. Despite facing the toughest challenges, I survived by relying on my inner strength, determination, and the courage to endure, all driven by my dreams.

I trusted in God, even when I had doubts. My survival has a greater purpose, and now I share my story with you. While I personally haven't considered suicide, it's devastating that countless children have lost their lives due to neglect, abuse, and other unbearable circumstances.

My mother passed away in June 1987. She developed breast cancer in Puerto Rico, but she was unaware and did not have health care to discover it early until she came to Atlanta.

She had a double mastectomy five years before, and doctors considered her cancer-free. This attribute can be traced back to other female members within the family, who also share it.

At the time she was 46 years of age; she passed away just days before her 47 birthdate, I loved her much and I still carry her overwhelming love for her children in my heart.

Mother's Day is tough, and though I cry about her absence, I know she lives in my heart.

My father passed away five years later in March of 1996, at age 52. He died of a heart attack just a month before my son was born. Our relationship was never the same.

My daughter was only a year old when he met her, but he never had the chance to meet our second child, who my wife was expecting.

My father was a source of pain for us and had multiple opportunities to be a better father, but he let us down and broke our trust too many times.

I had not seen my father in a few years since our last phone conversation, but a month before he got sick, I felt a strong connection with God.

In a dream, he told me to visit my father and ask for forgiveness, I was angry and confused because, deep down; I knew I no longer loved him.

Here I am once more questioning my creator.

Why are you telling me to ask my father to forgive me? In the hospital, my siblings and I shed tears together. It was not about his impending death, but about bidding farewell to our painful past.

On his deathbed, I hugged my father closely, while one of my sisters stepped out, creating a moment between me and the man who had caused us so much pain.

With a gentle voice, I asked my father to forgive me for not being the son he desired, despite the abuse and hatred he had caused.

My father and I met one last time when he was on his death bed. while one of my sisters stepped out, creating a moment between me and the man who had caused us so much hate and pain. With a gentle voice, I leaned in close and whispered to him that I was sorry I was not the man he wanted me to be. With tearful eyes he understood, this was our last conversation. He softly whispered with his last breath, you don't have to say that; I am the one who's sorry for how I treated you. That was the only time my father shed a tear and said I'm sorry.

With tears in my eyes, I stepped away from him, shocked that those were his last words before he passed away. He apologized and, as I walked away, I heard him take his final breath peacefully.

He remarried in the same year that he died, and tried to present his last wife as our mother, but we never embraced her.

Following his funeral, they cremated his remains and placed them in an urn, and I am unaware of its whereabouts.

None of his children cared to hold on to it, and it may have wandered around for a while. I believe his ashes were scattered in the Gulf of Mexico. He never had the burial he may have wanted and never saw his homeland again. But he had sealed his fate.

God helped me replace hate with love for my wife and children, and despite losing my mother and not having a father, I flourished.

"I forgive my father, but this does not mean I accepted his behavior or would ever trust him again. It means that I forgive him so that I can put all the pain behind me and continue my relentless pursuit to move forward and thrive".

In the Mirror of Life

I looked at the mirror of a life past and I saw a child abused, confused, and crying for hope. I suffered horror and anguish and lived a life of gender dysphoria. My life was chaos. Here I am at 62 years of age writing the story of my life and as I look back in the mirror, I see a transgender woman with lessons learned, proud with courage, strength, and determination. Never stop believing in yourself, and above all, love yourself unconditionally.

THE SIGNS OF AN
ABUSIVE PARENT

What are the traits of abusive parents?

My father scored 13 points on this list.

1. The Parent Uses Violence as a Form of Punishment
2. Consistently Makes Critical or Hurtful Comments
3. Humiliates the Child in Front of Other People
4. Is Sexually Inappropriate with the Child
5. Exposes Their Child to Inappropriate Sexual Content
6. Treats Their Child Like a Romantic Partner
7. Withholds Love from Their Children
8. Uses Manipulation to Get What They Want
9. The Parent's Anger Is Unpredictable
10. Withholds Basic Necessities
11. Targets Siblings Against One Another
12. Takes Financial Advantage of Their Child
13. Controls Their Child's Behavior
14. Uses Religion to Control a Child

HELPFUL RESOURCES

Suicide is devastating to family, friends, and community and can leave parents, siblings, classmates, and neighbors wondering if they could have prevented that teenager from turning to suicide.

Things that increase the risk of suicide among teens include:

1. Psychological disorders, depression, bipolar disorder, alcohol and drug abuse, sexual abuse, and physical, verbal, and mental abuse.
2. Feelings about hopelessness and worthlessness that often come with depression.
3. Previous suicide attempts.
4. Family history of depression or suicide.
5. Lack of a support network, poor relationships with parents or peers, and feelings of social isolation.
6. Struggling with their gender identity and/or sexuality in an unsupportive family or community.

The source for the data above came from www.kidshealth.org

ADDITIONAL RESOURCES

The National Child Abuse Hotline at 1-800-4-A-Child
(1-800-422-4453). https://nationalchildabusecoalition.org

Prevent Child Abuse - Together for Prevention National Conference
https://preventchildabuse.org/ Phone (312) 663-3520

National Suicide Prevention Hotline 988 Help is just one call away 24/7
https://988lifeline.org/

Behavioral Health Centers https://www.behavioralhealth-centers.com/
(855) 299-4472

Professional Therapy – BetterHelp https://www.betterhelp.com/

Offering positive coaching, caring, and counseling in Atlanta, GA,
Positive Psychology! https://www.rocksprings.biz/ (404) 721-7409

There are more resources online and in your local area; wherever you get
help, do it before it's too late.

ABOUT THE AUTHOR

Tamara Rivera is a passionate author and transgender rights advocate, was born in Rio Piedras, Puerto Rico. Moving to Chicago at a young age and later returning to Puerto Rico for a decade.

She faced a challenging journey through hardship and self-discovery, and embraced her true self, revealing her courage by coming out in September 2021. and legally changed her first name to Tamara by the end of the year.

Her memoir, Becoming Tamara, tells her powerful story of resilience, chronicling her journey through life's struggles and her path to authenticity. With a background in technology, she brings a unique perspective to her writing, weaving personal insights with broader messages of hope and acceptance.

Balancing her roles as an advocate, nail artist, and storyteller, Tamara's dedication shines through in her work, including her recent projects, which include publishing and revising multiple books. Her commitment to LGBTQ+ rights and inclusivity drives her work, as she shares her personal journey and the wisdom she's gained along the way. Passionate about fashion, beauty, and storytelling, Tamara Rivera is not only a voice for herself but an inspiration to countless others, exemplifying resilience, authenticity, and the transformative power of self-belief.